I AM a King

ANTONIO MAXWELL

Copyright © 2019 Antonio Maxwell Benton

All rights reserved. No part of this book may be reproduced in any form, stored in a retrieval system or transmitted in any form or by any means electronic, mechanical, photocopying or otherwise without the prior written permission from the author.

The purpose of the book is to tell the author's story and to encourage others. This book is not intended as a substitute for the advice of professionals. Please seek spiritual guidance and counselling from trained professionals as necessary. This book is a memoir that reflects the author's present recollections of experiences over time. Some events have been compressed, and some dialogue has been recreated. Photographs have been used by permission.

ISBN: 0-578-21810-0
ISBN-13: 978-0-578-21810-6

Layout and editing: Marsha A. Malcolm
Author photograph: Anthony Smith
Cover design: Bogdan Matei

Scriptures marked BSB are taken from the Holy Bible, Berean Study Bible, BSB. Copyright ©2016, 2018 by Bible Hub Used by Permission. All Rights Reserved Worldwide.

Scriptures marked ESV are from the ESV® Bible (The Holy Bible, English Standard Version®), copyright © 2001 by Crossway, a publishing ministry of Good News Publishers. Used by permission. All rights reserved.

Scriptures marked KJV are taken from the KING JAMES VERSION (KJV): KING JAMES VERSION, public domain.

Scriptures marked MON are taken from the MODERN ENGLISH VERSION (MON): Centenary Translation: THE NEW TESTAMENT IN MODERN ENGLISH by Helen Barrett Montgomery, 1924.

Scriptures marked NAS are taken from the NEW AMERICAN STANDARD (NAS): Scripture taken from the NEW AMERICAN STANDARD BIBLE®, copyright© 1960, 1962, 1963, 1968, 1971, 1972, 1973, 1975, 1977, 1995 by The Lockman Foundation. Used by permission.

Scriptures marked NIV are taken from the Holy Bible, New International Version®, NIV®. Copyright © 1973, 1978, 1984, 2011 by Biblica, Inc.™ Used by permission of Zondervan. All rights reserved worldwide. www.zondervan.com The "NIV" and "New International Version" are trademarks registered in the United States Patent and Trademark Office by Biblica, Inc.™

Scriptures marked NKJV are from the New King James Version®. Copyright © 1982 by Thomas Nelson. Used by permission.

PRAISE FOR *I AM A KING*

"Antonio shares his life without reserve. A raw openness on his life of trauma and triumph is an enlightenment for the soul. Antonio's life is filled with lessons we cannot neglect to learn. This book reminds us of our true strength that is only experienced through perseverance. Prepare yourself to be blessed with lessons that manifest King and Queenship."

Kevin Stallworth
Yeoman Chief Petty Officer, United States Navy

"*I AM a King*, written with passion, fervor and sincerity, takes us inside the heart, mind and soul of a young boy who was supposed to fail. Antonio's story is a must-read as it brings a dynamic of hope, faith and believing to a level that will reach in and touch the innermost parts of the heart that even the hardest of hearts can't ignore. Open your mind and heart as Antonio shares his story of how Christ changed his life. You'll be glad you did. Captivating!"

Aretha Weaver
Flight Attendant/PR Specialist

"Antonio's book *I AM a King* is an open book of his life for all to see and learn from. He takes you on a journey of love, hurts, victories and defeats... all the while being engrafted into his kingship as he walks out God's destiny for his life."

D. Marshall
Retired US Navy Petty Officer 1st Class

"Being a King is trusting and having the faith that God will do everything He promised. This book is an inspiration to anyone who reads it. Mr. Benton shows how his faith in God stood strong in every way even in the lowest times in his life. He truly shares what it takes to be a King by serving a King!"

Natalie Kohn-Spikes
Educator

"Amazing read!!! This book shall touch and transform the lives of many. Antonio is indeed a picture of good success. Seeing the things that he had to overcome, over these many years, shows the true grace of God!! *I AM a King* will be a major tool, used by God, for many years to come."

Min. J. McKay, Diplomats In Training LLP

DEDICATION

This book is dedicated to the Benton, Peterman, Holt, Farve, Rieux, and Kay families.

Thank all of you for loving me the best way you knew how. Please know that the roles you played in my life — good or bad — have helped make me into the man of God I am today.

To my sons Kai and Kaden – I love you boys with all my heart. God gave you guys to me and I gave you back to Him. You are His!!

To my one and only daughter Sophia – God doesn't make mistakes. God chose you for our family for a reason and a purpose. What a blessing you are to me. Daddy loves you so much.

To my ex-wife – thank you for 11 amazing years of marriage. You will forever have a special place in my heart. Thank you for partnering up with me as parents should in raising these wonderful kids with me.

To my cousin Jason McKay aka LP – thank you for encouraging me year after year to write this book. May God get the glory.

To De Mont Mitchell, Darrell Marshall, Santonio Williams, Kevin Stallworth, Shavon Jacobs, Nathaniel Harvey, and Jose Martinez. Thank you mighty men of God for all your love and support over the years. If it wasn't for your continuous prayer, encouragement, love, and support, there is no telling where I would be. I love you guys.

Last but not least, to my mentor Minister Holmes. I know you are in heaven looking down on me. Thank you for letting God use you to help mold me into the man of God I am today. I love you, man. RIP.

Contents

Dedication v
Acknowledgments 1
Introduction 5
1 The Generational Curse 7
2 The Struggle Is Real 11
3 The Favor of God 15
4 Moving On 27
5 My Conversion 31
6 Back to School 39
7 Adoption #1 43
8 Adoption #2 49
9 Before The Storm 53
10 My Road to Damascus Experience 65
11 My Eyes Are Opened 71
12 Coming Out of the Wilderness 81
13 God's Love 85
14 The Devil Is After Your Mind 89
15 The Devil – The Accuser of the Brethren 93
16 The Healing Process 97
17 My Next Chapter 105
18 Purpose 109
19 The Only Way We Are Going to Make It 117
About the Author 124

Acknowledgments

To my Lord and Savior Jesus Christ, for leading and guiding my hands and mind to write this book. I know You allow us to go through things for a reason. I thank You for giving me the strength to weather all the storms I've gone through in my life. If it wasn't for the Holy Spirit living inside my heart, I don't know where I would be.

To my ex-wife, for the love and support you gave me over our 11-year marriage. Although we didn't make it to the Promised Land as a couple, our journey together is still not over.

To my beautiful kids Kai, Kaden, and Sophia, for loving Daddy unconditionally.

To my mother – thank you for always encouraging me to be the man God has called me to be, and for praying with me in all my endeavors.

To momma Pearl Peterman – Jason and I used to joke growing up that you had a seat waiting for you right next to Jesus. Thank you for exemplifying the love of Christ Jesus so hard that two young boys who didn't know Christ could recognize it at a young age. Your love has made a mark on my life that could never be erased. I love you so much for that.

To Donna Holt, my very first adopted mother. You saw something in me that I didn't see in myself at a young age. You sowed a seed of greatness into me, and now you are seeing the harvest of it right before your eyes. I can't express how much your love meant to me. There aren't words out there that can explain it, either. Just always know that I'm grateful for all you did in my life. I love you!

To my brother and sister, Jermaine and Shamika – even though we grew apart over the years, I never stopped praying for you guys. I will always love you. You will forever have a special place in my heart.

To my father – even though you were never there for me, I don't hold a grudge against you! I forgive you!! I love you.

To my cousin Jason, thank you for always being there for me and lending an open ear to me. This road wasn't easy, brother, but we made it, cuz. Love you, man!

To my brother Paul – thank you for loving me like I was your real brother. I was nothing like any of the people you grew up around and you never made me feel any differently. Thank you, brother. I love you for the love you showed me.

To my brother Stephen Peterman – thank you for not never judging me by the color of my skin and my dysfunctional background. Even though we grew apart over the years, you still have a special place in my heart, brother. I hope one day we can reunite. Love you, bro!

To my brother in Christ, Kevin Stallworth – thank you for all your love and support in the most trying time of my life. You were God-sent in my life for that season. I will forever be indebted to you, brother. Love you, man!

To my brother in Christ, Darrell Marshall – I wouldn't be the man of God I am today if it wasn't for the example you walked out in front on me. You are a true definition of a real man of God and true friend. Love you, man.

To my brother Nathaniel Harvey – I just want to say I love you, man. You walked through the storm with me, holding my hand, encouraging me after every step we took. We are brothers for life.

To my brother De Mont Mitchell – thank for being who God called you to be: a freaking comedian! Your jokes helped me get through whatever situation I was dealing with at the time! Thanks for keeping me laughing.

To my brothers and sister in Christ, Jose, Tonio, Marcus, Aretha – thank you guys for all your love and support over the years. I love you guys dearly!

To my brother William Lavant – thanks for all your love and support. I want you to know that you're a genius!! Thank you for seeing something in me that I didn't even see in myself. Thank you for believing in me. Much love, bro!

To my pastors Russ and Debbie Austin, for all your love and support. Pastor Russ, you didn't have to take time out to talk to me, but you did. That really meant a lot to me. I want you to know that I appreciate all you guys do for the Southpoint Community Church. Love you guys!

To my brothers at Jun's Barbershop: Thomas, Jason, and VJ – thank you guys for your continuous support. You guys are my brothers for life. God bless!

To AMAX GANG – thanks for all your love and support through social media. This book wouldn't be possible if it wasn't for your support! Love you guys!

To LaFonda Middleton, for helping me walk through the journey of publishing my first book. Your book encouraged me and helped make my book possible. Thank you!

To pastor Jeffery Reed – thank you for the foundation that you laid for me as a new believer. I love you and First Lady Tina Reed. Powerhouse of Deliverance will always be my home.

To Mr. Harry Farve, you are the earthly father I never had. Thank you for all your love and support over the years. Love you, man.

To Joyce Reiux, I first want to say I love you. The unconditional love you showed to me over the years is priceless. You are a jewel in my life. Keep letting your light shine so brightly in a world full of darkness.

To my aunt Evelyn, thank you for letting God lead you when you decided to take me in. I will never forget all you've done for me. I love you more than you will ever know.

INTRODUCTION

This is a book about a young black kid from a small town in Mississippi who was dealt a bad hand in life. When you look at the statistics, the odds of him making it out of the hood were slim to none. If you look at the dysfunction down the line of his family tree from generation to generation, you would've never imagined this kid to even be writing a book today. If you knew this kid growing up, you would surely agree; even if you *didn't* know him.

Well, you're about to read the story of how God hand-picked this kid out of the hands of the enemy. How He placed him among people from different walks of life who loved him like their own. How He saved him from a life of drugs, alcohol, and crime, and how He kept him from an almost-certain death.

Now buckle your seatbelt; you're in for quite a ride. This is the story of Antonio Benton, the 38-year-old father, friend, ex-husband, servant, and son of a King.

1 THE GENERATIONAL CURSE

Born to a military father and a submissive mother in Gulfport, Mississippi, I was the second of three children. My dad was in the Army and my mother was a stay-at-home mom. My dad was stationed in Germany for a while until he got in some trouble and was shipped back to Mississippi. He was discharged from the military for violating the drug policy. That was where his habits started, and they unfortunately continue to this day.

For my entire life, my father has struggled with drug abuse and alcoholism, and has been in and out of jail. Because of his inability to stay clean and out of jail, I have never had a relationship with him. Throughout my life, I would see him around town riding a bike, looking for ways to make money. I would speak to him and sometimes he would hold a conversation with me — nothing serious, just surface talk — and then he was off to his normal everyday hustle. I never asked why he was in the situation he was in, because I didn't understand at the time. I just knew he was my dad and I was always taught to respect my elders.

I can remember times when I, as a teenager, would spot him riding his bike through town. How embarrassed I was to see him, knowing the life he was living. Sometimes I acted like I didn't see him, hoping he wouldn't stop to talk to me. Still, I was never disrespectful towards him in any way.

Other kids would make fun of me when he passed by, riding his bike in the neighborhood. Yes, it did bother me, but there was nothing I could do or say to change the situation. All I knew was that he was my father and I was his son.

My mother was a submissive wife to my father. She didn't work while my dad was in the military. My mom has always been a very compassionate and loving person. She was always very protective over her children. I guess you could say she had that 'momma bear' mentality.

Once she and my dad separated because of his neglect towards our family, she was forced to work and find other means to provide for us. Thank God we had my grandmother there to help support us, as well. My grandmother was the foundation of our family. She was what you would call the 'Big Momma' of the family. She was hard-working, loving, and could be tough when needed to be. She was the glue that kept what little of a family we had together.

When I say *family*, I mean my aunt, her three kids, and us. My aunt lived in Ohio at the time with one of her sons. My grandmother was helping take care of her other two kids while helping support us. We all lived together in a three-bedroom home in Bay Saint Louis, Mississippi. My grandmother worked a job while my mom was always in and out of jobs. We were on every government assistant program known to man (food stamps, Medicaid, WIC, financial assistance, etc.). We were renting the house we lived in, and it was infested with roaches and rats.

Even though we were getting food stamps, we barely ever had food because of the size of our family. My mother and grandmother struggled terribly trying to provide for everyone. We struggled with just keeping the basic necessities in the home. There were many times when my mother and grandmother couldn't afford to pay the light bill, and we went days without electricity in the house. When it was time for school to start, we wore hand-me-downs; we never had haircuts, and we never had the right supplies for school.

We got picked on at school every day, so we felt like we had to fight a lot to defend ourselves from other kids. It also taught us as siblings how to stick together no matter what. We had this mentality that if you messed with one, you messed with us all.

2 THE STRUGGLE IS REAL

My grandmother started dating a man she had met. He was a home-builder. He had a crew that helped him build homes in the city. My grandmother came across some funds somehow, so she bought some land in the city next to ours called Waveland. She hired her friend to build us a home. We were excited about the fact that we were having a new home built. We were also happy to know we were moving out of the city in which we had experienced so much trauma.

They started building the house and it was coming along fine. We started packing up to move into our new home. Then without any warning, there was a shift in the plans. I still don't know to this day what happened, but my grandmother's friend the builder magically disappeared. He left town and no one knew where he was. We never saw him again. The problem with that was the house wasn't finished being built!!

As I mentioned earlier, we had already started packing to move. The home was being built with wood. The bad news was that it was in the middle of the woods. It turned out that it had major issues we didn't have the money to fix. The toilet didn't work; anytime we used the bathroom, we had to pour water down the toilet so it would flush. We didn't have a water heater, so we didn't have hot water. We didn't have an A/C unit. In the winter, we used space heaters and the oven to stay warm. In the summer, we used fans to stay cool.

We didn't have a washer or dryer. My mom went to the laundromat once a month to do laundry. If we couldn't go to the laundromat, we washed clothes by hand and dried them next to the oven.

The house was heavily infested with rats, roaches, and other bugs. I can remember my siblings and I would be sleeping at night and you could hear rats running across the ceiling. Our sewage system was at the back of the house, so you could smell sewage every time you stepped outside.

The house next to ours had a mini farm with goats, chickens, and roosters. We had fun messing with the animals. There was this one goat that was mean as heck. I remember one day going next door to mess with him. I was pulling on his horns and he was good and mad. I turned around to walk away and he butted me right in my butt cheek. I was so angry and in *so* much pain. When I turned around to look at him, he had this look on his face like he was laughing at me. I was mad as heck, but it was pretty funny at the same time. I learned my lesson from that. I never messed with that goat ever again. I tell you, other than tormenting the animals, nothing was fun about living next to that mini farm.

The struggle was even worse in our "NEW" house. When the light bill didn't get paid on time and we lost electricity, we didn't have enough lamps to

The ghetto isn't a place; I tell people all the time that being from the ghetto means you learn how to survive with what you have.

keep the whole house lit. Imagine what that was like in the dark, in the middle of the woods with little lighting. True, it wasn't fun, but we made the best of it. We were used to living in unfamiliar environments like that. The ghetto isn't a place; I tell people all the time that being from the ghetto means you learn how to survive with what you have.

3 THE FAVOR OF GOD

Shortly after we moved into our "NEW" house, my aunt moved down from Ohio with her son, my cousin. She moved into her own home and her two kids moved out of our house and in with her. Now there were only my two siblings, myself, my mother, and my grandmother living in our house.

It was hard for my siblings and me to get used to being without our cousins. We would visit them every day at their new house. Their home situation was a lot better than ours, so we would go there often to escape the reality at home. We had to start at a new school, where nothing changed for us in terms of the treatment we got from the other kids. We got picked on even more and had to fight more every day. I came to the conclusion that kids are just cruel. I didn't understand how kids could hate you so much just because you didn't look or dress like them, or because you didn't have the same material things they had. It didn't make sense to me, but it didn't take long for our presence to be known around there. We were skilled at fighting, and people learned the hard way.

Out of the blue, my grandma started getting sick and we couldn't figure out what was going on with her. After a month of fighting sickness, she was diagnosed with cancer and later a brain tumor. We were devastated! She couldn't work anymore. Her health started deteriorating at an alarming rate. Before long, she was bedridden. She couldn't get out the bed to go to the bathroom by herself; we had to do everything for her. She started losing her hair.

As you can imagine, we were all in a state of shock! It's not easy having to see the person we had known as the big provider for our family in that kind of shape. We didn't know how we would make it if we lost her. We were afraid and exhausted all at the same time. It was a lot of work caring for her, especially because she had originally weighed around 400 pounds.

Can you imagine being a ten-year-old kid, seeing the most influential person in your life dying right in front of you? My grandmother had always been such a strong woman. She made it happen for our family and she did whatever it took for us to be okay.

Her health started declining at an even more rapid rate each day, and we kind of expected what was coming next. My grandmother ended up dying at home. At that time in my life, I had never experienced that kind of hurt or pain before. My grandmother was the toughest woman I had ever met in my life. Without her, we didn't know what we were going to do.

My mother was totally lost without her mom – the person who had been there for her basically her whole life. I could see in my mother's face that she wasn't in a good place mentally. She took it very hard! She didn't know how to process it, so she turned to drugs and alcohol.

She was dating this man who lived with us at times. He was a pretty cool guy; he just always had a hard time finding a job. My grandmother hadn't liked him, but my mother kept him around. When her mother died, he moved in. He and my mother were always drinking and doing drugs. They would do the drugs in the bedroom with the door closed. We always knew what they were doing in the room.

My mom's habits started getting worse. She and her boyfriend would go out to the club at night and leave us home alone. I can remember being so scared to go to sleep at night. You would hear animals and all kinds of noises outside of the house. I remember waking up the next morning so excited that I made it through the night. My brother and sister didn't have a problem at all going to sleep; I guess I was just the scared sibling.

I can remember Christmas coming around the corner and I was so excited. I always loved the holidays, because that was the only time we came together as a family. That was the only time everyone around me was happy and excited. I simply loved the holidays. We usually would get only a couple pieces of clothes for Christmas and sometimes something like a bike. This Christmas was different though; miraculously, my grandmother had left some money to my mother when she died. We were able to have a Christmas with presents that year. We were also able to get a real

Christmas tree that year instead of one we cut down ourselves out of the woods. We were so excited and sad at the same time – excited because we were able to get presents and sad because my grandmother wasn't able to celebrate with us. Even though she was gone, her gift allowed us to have the best Christmas ever!!

The holidays passed by, but the struggles were still there. The city we lived in was actually the city where my dad's family lived. My mother and my dad's mom didn't get along for whatever reason. We occasionally went to my paternal grandmother's house to hang out. My dad had a brother who was a little closer in age to us. My siblings and I started hanging out with my uncle. All of the men on my dad's side of the family — at least the ones we knew — were alcoholics, thieves, and drug users. With my uncle being older, he had a lot of influence on us, so we got into burglarizing houses and shoplifting. Thank God we never got caught. Looking back, I can say without a doubt that if we as parents don't give our children the correct guidance, they will get guidance from *somewhere,* and it might not be the type of influence we agree with.

When kids with no positive guidance grow up in a poverty-stricken environment, they develop a poverty mindset. That's a recipe for disaster!! Poverty drains your soul and leaves you feeling empty inside. As a kid living that life where everywhere you look there are signs of hopelessness, you start believing there is no hope for your life. So as soon as someone gives you attention that looks like a sign of love, you gravitate towards that person. That's how the enemy uses the wrong people to influence people's lives in a negative way. That's why it was so easy for my uncle to influence us into doing the things we knew were wrong.

There was a baseball league in our town that all the kids played in. I can't recall how my brother and I were able to pay to participate in the league. We started playing baseball and we were both pretty good at it. I ended up being on the same team as my uncle Jason. Jason is my mother's brother by her father. I actually didn't like Jason originally; he

>
> If we as parents don't give our children the correct guidance, they will get guidance from *somewhere...*

would go around telling people I was his nephew as a way of making fun of me. I didn't like it because I was older than him. Later in this story, you will see the important role he ended up playing in my life.

Playing baseball turned out to be a positive outlet for all of us. We still were doing some bad things, but nothing too serious that we could get in a lot of trouble for. We ended up playing that season and we had lots of fun.

The next year I was switched to another team. My coach was a white man named Alfred Holt. His son Jared played on the team as the catcher. The Holt family were pretty wealthy, and they owned a restaurant. I was a very good baseball player, so my coach started taking a special interest in me. I also became close friends with his son. The Holts started allowing me to come to their house, and the next thing I knew, I was spending nights there to escape the reality of what was going on at home.

As time went by, they started treating my like I was their second son. This family really started exposing me to things I never would've experienced if I hadn't met them. We went on trips and spent holidays together.

Mr. Holt was a big-bellied man with a ruddy complexion and red hair. I really don't think he cared too much for me, but he tolerated me because his wife favored me. He would make fun of black people to his son. He would often use the N word when making comments about black people. He would never do it around us, only to his son when we weren't around. Later, Jared would tell us what his father had said. It really didn't matter to me, because he wasn't doing it directly to me. I was a kid; what was I going to do? Plus, his wife was the boss in that house, and she loved me. The next season, I was on their baseball team again.

By the time I was 12 years old, my siblings were smoking cigarettes and not long after that, they began smoking weed and drinking. I remember not wanting to try cigarettes, because I understood what the cycle of smoking cigarettes led to. I wasn't trying to go down that road. My siblings' behavior really started getting out of control. I was starting to get sick and tired of our situation at the time. Our living conditions, my mom doing drugs, and my siblings' behavior were all starting to weigh on me. I knew there was more to life than what I was seeing right in front of me.

I can remember sitting down one day and saying to myself, "I don't want to live the rest of my like this." I believe that is when God heard my cry and grabbed a hold of my hand and started directing my path.

I left my mom's house and started living with my aunt – the one who had moved down from Ohio. The living conditions were a lot better than my previous situation. My aunt worked two jobs to support us. I started going back and forth between the Holts' house and my aunt's house.

The next baseball season started and that year my uncle Jason was on the team with me. We started developing a strong bond with each other. I started staying at his house from time to time and at that point we became inseparable. I started playing my second year of Pee Wee football at the age of 12 years old. Jason and I just so happened to end up on the same team again. I played the position of running back. I was really good at it, too.

On our football team, I met a white boy by the name of Stephen Peterman. His dad was one of our coaches. Stephen had a big family and his mom and dad owned a convenience store, liquor store, and laundromat. The rumor in the neighborhood was that Mr. Peterman didn't like black people. I never saw any signs of that being true about him. All I know is he loved me as if I was his own son. I became best friends with Stephen. I begin staying with them on and off, while also splitting time with the Holt family, at my uncle Jason's home, and at my aunt's house, ever so often.

What a coincidence that the Holt and Peterman family businesses were located on the same street. They knew each other very well. They both sent their children to the same private school. While playing pee wee football, I also met a black boy by the name of Paul and his dad, Mr. Harry Farve, who would come to play a big role in my life later on.

Stephen and I started working for his dad making $3.00 an hour cleaning the stores. The Petermans really wanted me to go to St. Stanislaus's (the private Catholic school their children attended) and they had connections to get me in on a scholarship. At $300.00 for school tuition, this was a big blessing from God. I could see that, even though I didn't know God or Jesus at that time. I ended up going to St. Stanislaus from seventh to tenth grade. I was a standout athlete in football, basketball, baseball, and track.

While playing sports at St. Stanislaus, I became really good friends with Paul. I was the brother Paul never had. Our relationship developed fast. His dad Mr. Harry allowed me to stay at his home from time to time. Now I was in-between staying with the Holts, the Petermans, my aunt, and the Farves.

After my tenth grade year at St. Stanislaus, I started feeling like I didn't want to be a student there anymore. I decided to transfer to the school I would have gone to if I hadn't met all those different families. I left St. Stanislaus and I enrolled in Bay High Public School.

When I started going to Bay High, my relationship with my uncle Jason got stronger, since he was already enrolled there. We were star football players on the team and two of the most popular guys at school. It was funny how the tables had turned from me being the kid always being picked on to the most popular, sought-after student. God was in control! The bible does say, "… the last shall be first, and the first last: for many be called, but few chosen." (Matt. 20:16, KJV)

4 MOVING ON

By this time, I wasn't seeing the Holt and Peterman families as often, because I was going to another school. St. Stanislaus and Bay High were cross-town rivals. Now I was competing against my two best friends, Paul and Stephen. I would go to visit Mr. and Mrs. Peterman at times and always kept in contact with them. It was the same with the Holt family. I'm that person who is very grateful when anyone does anything for me. It's important to continually show people that we appreciate them, and I made it a point of my duty to do just that.

While at Bay High, I started dating a girl who later introduced me to her grandparents, who also formed a

>
> **It's important to continually show people that we appreciate them. I made it a point of my duty to do just that.**

bond with me. At this time, I was basically staying at my aunt's, and occasionally at Mr. Harry's house. My junior year had gone by and I excelled on the football field and in the classroom.

My senior year was supposed to be my breakout year in football. I was being highly recruited by major colleges. My girlfriend's grandparents allowed me to stay at their home from time to time. My senior year was about to start and I felt like I needed to be stationary so that I could focus on football. I knew my ticket to making it "out the hood for good" was in getting a football scholarship. My defensive coach and his wife (a white couple) asked if I wanted to come live with them. I felt like that would be best for me, so I said yes and moved in. Now, for once in my life, I was in one stable environment, and able to focus primarily on football and academics.

That year started off on a good track! In the third game of the season, I hurt my knee and it sidelined me for one game. I finished my senior year of football. I had a great season and many major colleges were after me, but because of my size and weight, they wanted me to go to a community college first so I could get some experience and size on my small body frame. A coach from Pearl River Community College came to my home to visit me and watch my film. The college wasn't far from home, so I decided to sign up with them for a scholarship. I went to college to play football and excel academically. Because of my frustration with the coaches, my mind was distracted from the academic side of things. I felt like the coaches sold me a dream to come to their school, because once I got there they didn't give me an opportunity to play the position they recruited me for. I got a lot of playing time, but I wasn't happy at the position I was forced to play. After the football season was over, I left school and went back home.

5 MY CONVERSION

It was then that I joined the US Navy. I went to boot camp and I started cutting hair on the side. That wasn't my original job, but I knew a little about cutting hair even though I had never "cut a head" before. My uncle Jason had been the neighborhood barber while we were in high school. I guess I picked up on it by just being with him and watching him cut.

When I reported to my ship in Pascagoula, Mississippi upon finishing "A" school – additional technical training for Navy recruits after boot camp – I was told that my ship was leaving for a six-month deployment in 16 days. We were deployed to Europe.

While on deployment, I did some things that any 19-year-old who had never been out of his home state would've done; things that I'm not so proud of today, but when you're young you do things without thinking. I was single with money, and didn't have a worry in the world. I would go to clubs with my boys, drink, and have sex with multiple women. I felt like it filled a void in my life, but I can tell you from experience that there is a void only God can fill. I tried to fill it with sin, but eventually, I came to realize it was God I needed. I just thank God that I'm alive, healthy, and able to share this story with you.

When I came back from deployment, I called Jason, bragging about the things I had done and all the things I had seen. Jason had gone off to college in Alabama. I called him up and while we were on the phone, he started telling me about this great experience that had taken place in his life. He told me that he had accepted Jesus as his Lord and savior. He was so excited as he told me about this Jesus of his and he proceeded to tell me how I could be saved.

I remember thinking to myself, *Things are going pretty good in my life without this Jesus; how much better could things get with this Jesus?* And I saw it as a way of escaping going to hell. So on April 14, 2001, I accepted Jesus Christ in my heart, over the phone. "[T]hat if you confess with your mouth Jesus is Lord, and believe in your heart that God has raised Him from the dead, you will be saved…." (Rom. 10:9, MON)

I found out quickly that it was more than just missing hell, it's a lifestyle, and I was up for the challenge. From that day on, I never looked back. I started going to church, meeting other brothers in Christ, and became a part of a ministry onboard the ship.

In 2005, I got orders to go to Jacksonville, Florida and was stationed on board the USS John F. Kennedy. My job was merging with another job that I didn't care for. The Navy allowed us to choose another job for which we were qualified. I qualified for three other jobs in the navy. Guess what position was available? You guessed right! The barber job (ship serviceman).

On the Kennedy, I helped out in a ministry that led many people to Christ. The Kennedy is an aircraft carrier that held over 4,000 people when we deployed. It was like a small city! There was a lot of demonic activity going on there. I ended up running the barbershop on the ship. While on the ship I met a guy who introduced me to an awesome church called the Church of Jacksonville. I became a member, and then I was introduced to a man by the name of Minister Holmes. He later became my mentor.

***

My life really took a change the day I was introduced to the woman who would become my wife all of 15 months later – a beautiful, smart, awesome woman who doesn't want to be named here.

It didn't take long for me to figure out that she would be my wife. She was strong in all my weaknesses and I was strong in all of hers. I married the love of my life; a virgin. When I met her, I said to myself, "I've never met a woman like this before in my life." I knew I had to make her my wife and that was my ultimate goal. My circle of friends, a.k.a. my 'holy of holies' all approved of her, so it was a no brainer. She was amazing to me and amazing to everyone around her. Young; so sweet; so innocent; so delicate, and so compassionate. The anointing of God was so evident on her that it confused people of the opposite sex. If she talked to males, they would often get the wrong impression of her. She was very aware that she should not look men in the eyes, because she never wanted to give the wrong impression that she was flirting with them. She was the most honest person I had ever met. She was my wife, my jewel, and my prize.

I can remember thinking how I couldn't live without her and that she was so special to me! I was a little over-protective of her, because I didn't want anyone to hurt her in anyway. That's when I knew I had to "put a ring on it" – and soon! I proposed and she said "Yes!" I married her in 2006.

Life was grand! Little did I know or realize when we were dating, that my wife liked to share *all* her thoughts and emotions. It caught me off-guard once we got married and to be honest, I didn't know how to handle it, simply because I had never had to show emotion and never really knew how to be that kind of person for anyone in my life. I was very unskilled in that area, but I figured I would learn as we grew together as a married couple. I can admit I got better with time. My wife saw some progress, but she needed more. So she started getting that emotional support from her female friends. I was okay with that, but in my mind my goal was to help her become stronger as a person and to not get so wrapped up in her emotions and feelings. I admit that I felt she was a little fragile, so I tried in my own way to toughen her up somewhat, because I knew how vicious people in the world could be. I knew there were people out there who would try and take advantage of her, and I didn't want that to happen.

God called me out of active duty military in 2008. That was the most trying time in our life as a married couple, because God didn't tell us what to do or where to go, so we just looked for the open doors and tried to walk through every door that opened, seeking the face of God. We tried moving out of Jacksonville to Orlando and it didn't work out for us. We had no jobs and we were running out of money. We packed up our bags and moved back to Jacksonville to my mother-in-law's house. Out of fear and nothing happening for us as far as a job was concerned, I tried to get back into active duty military. God didn't allow it to happen, but He did open up another door for me to get into the military reserves. I ended up getting a security job after being unemployed for a whole year.

Let me tell you something, when God directs you to do something and you step out on faith, don't allow fear to set up camp in your mind and detour you. God honored our decision to step out on faith and He gave us grace when we allowed fear to come in. If God said it, you better believe He is going to make provisions for wherever He is trying to get you to go or until He works out whatever He is trying to work out of you. He does this so that He can get you to where He is trying to take you. The Reserves gave us a means of income to be able to get some money and get back on our feet.

Now here is when the second greatest thing we experienced as a married couple and the third greatest thing I experienced in my life happened. In the midst of the storms going on in our life, God spoke to my wife and told her that it was time for us to have a baby. He

When God directs you to do something and you step out on faith, don't allow fear to set up camp in your mind and detour you.

confirmed it to me later, so we got in agreement and made it happen. On July 29, 2009, my first son was born into the world. What a joy and blessing! God then blessed us to be able to move into our own place.

6 BACK TO SCHOOL

In 2010, God blessed my wife with a teaching job. She had worked so hard, and had gone through so much to pass all her tests so that she could get her teacher certification.

Just when we didn't think things could get any better, the fourth greatest thing in my life happened to me. In January of 2011, God spoke to my wife's heart again and said we should have another baby. She told me what she felt God was saying to her and it didn't take God long to confirm it to me.

In June 2011, I started going to barber school courtesy of the Post-9/11 GI Bill. I had been saying that I was going to get my barber's license for a long time, but in God's timing, the door just swung open and the opportunity was staring me in the face. The Post-9/11 GI Bill paid 100% of my tuition and paid me a monthly housing allowance.

On October 9, 2011 my second son was born. What a joy it was seeing him for the first time. He looked just like my first son. On May 23, 2012, I finished barber school with a 4.0 GPA. On June 4, 2012 I started attending phlebotomy school. On August 18, 2012 we had a formal graduation for barber school and I was the speaker in front of around 300 students, teachers, family, and friends.

From the day I got saved, my prayer going forward was that my whole family would be saved. I'm glad to report that my mother, sister, and brother are all saved. We all have a plan, purpose, and destiny for our lives, but we can't get there without Jesus as your co-pilot. He leads and directs us every step of the way. We just have to be obedient and follow His directions. We make wrong turns and get off the path at times, but He knows how to get us back on the right path. That is how I live my life, confident that "all things work together for good to those who love God, to those who are called according to his purpose." (Rom. 8:28, NAS) If you know you love God and are called according to His purpose, then this scripture is for you too. Now believe it.

7 ADOPTION #1

I graduated from phlebotomy school with honors. I started working in a barbershop, but it didn't work out. I brought over the clientele I had established cutting out of the house some time earlier, but I needed to build up my customer base because my booth rent was expensive. Unfortunately, my clientele wasn't growing quickly enough. I still had money left from the Post-9/11 GI Bill, so I decided to enroll into medical assistance school at Keiser University. I ended up getting hired at the place I did my externship for the medical assistant program. I still had to finish my classes for my degree portion of the medical assistant program. I worked part time at a local spine center while I finished my classes. I was blessed, because the Post-9/11 GI Bill also paid me a housing allowance while I went to school.

My wife and I had talked about adopting when we first met. She shared with me then that when she was only five years old, God had put a desire in her heart to adopt an Asian baby. I was cool with it, because with all the families that had participated in raising me, I felt like I had basically been adopted myself, and I wanted to be able to give back. I was in total agreement with the idea.

In April 2014, my wife told me that she felt like it was time to start the process. We decided to do a domestic adoption, which means we planned to carry out the process within the US. We decided to try and adopt a baby of a different ethnicity, since we felt strongly about adding some diversity to our family. My wife started doing her research as usual, and before we knew it we were connected with a well-known agency. We had to put together a portfolio of our family, just to give the birth parents a kind-of glimpse into what kind of family we were. We put it together and submitted it.

If you don't know, you know now: adoptions are *very* expensive, and 90% of the people who adopt don't have the money to afford the process. As a result, people do fundraisers, take out loans, apply for grants, and use their own money to fund it. After going through the process, I understand why it's so expensive. The agency has to get paid; the birth parent(s) get(s) paid, and the lawyer has to get paid. When you look at it, it all makes sense. Is it right? I wouldn't say that, but it makes sense.

Now we were all set and ready to adopt! The agency started showing our book to birth moms. Let me interject here that our book was amazingly put together by my wife. If anyone looked at it, they would've wanted to pick us as parents from the start. Guess what?? Around three weeks later, my wife gets an email in the middle of the night saying we've been matched with a birth mom. The birth mom was giving birth the very next day in Gainesville, Florida, just an hour and a half away. We needed to meet them there that morning.

We were so excited and scared at the same time. We didn't expect to get matched so quickly. We were more excited than anything else, though. The baby had a white mom and a black dad.

We got up in the morning, gathered up our baby bags and car seat, and drove to Gainesville. Upon arrival, we met up with our adoption agency representative. Unfortunately, we missed the delivery, but we were happy to have made it there safely. This was all new to us, so we really didn't know how to feel or act. We walked into the room to meet our birth mom and new baby girl. Like I said, we didn't know how to feel, and it all felt so weird to me.

The mother loved us and was ready to sign over her rights and move on with her life. Of course, the devil wasn't going to let us off the hook that fast. There was a problem, and it was the birth father. He had a problem with the baby being adopted by a black family. He said that he experienced abuse when he was young by his grandmother, who was black, so he didn't want a black family adopting his baby. He didn't even want to meet us while we were at the hospital. The agency felt like he didn't do what he was supposed to do before the birth. If he decided to fight the adoption, they expected that he would lose. He didn't end up signing the papers that day, but my wife and I walked out of the hospital with a new baby girl.

It all felt so weird having this new baby with whom we had no physical connection. That poor baby screamed from the time we got her home until the time she left our home. We were really trying to bond with her as a family, but for some reason she was very fussy all the time. It was a little bit frustrating because we couldn't figure out why she was crying so much. Her crying made us wonder if she was experiencing withdrawal from something. We decided to stop giving her the breast milk from her birth mom and things seemed to get a little better. We finally came to a conclusion that maybe she had fetal alcohol syndrome. We can't confirm that, but that's what our instinct told us.

The father wanted to fight for the child if we were going to be the ones adopting her. The agency felt like it would've been worth all the extra money to fight against it, but the truth was that we would have been the ones paying the extra fees, and we knew we couldn't afford it. We agreed that it was best we let her go. We had her for six weeks and then she was gone.

We knew we had made the right decision letting her go, even though it was a hard one to make. When the day came for her to get picked up, to say we were sad would be an understatement. We really didn't allow ourselves to get attached to her because truly we really didn't know if the situation was going to work out for us in the end. We felt like we explained the process that was going on well with our boys who were five and three years old at the time. In the end, we were just thankful that God was able to use us to be a blessing to the baby girl for six weeks.

She was adopted by a different family the following week. I guess they met with the birth dad's approval. We looked at it as a blessing that God was able to use us in the situation. We were obedient in playing our role so that she could get to the right family. Through it all, we had to continue to remind ourselves that all things work together for the good for those who love God and called according to His purpose.

8 ADOPTION #2

I ended up graduating from Keiser in June 2014 with my degree. I began working full-time at the local spine center.

At that time, my wife and I were still on the hunt for our baby girl. We had two boys of our own, and we wanted a little girl to balance out all the testosterone in our family. We didn't know what the future held, but we were determined to continue to trust God, no matter what. We had many people praying for us and believing God on our behalf. Time started passing by and we entertained a couple of situations, but nothing happened. Then in November 2014, we got a call from the adoption agency about a situation for an African

American baby. God had already spoken to us about opening our mind to whatever He wanted to do with us in this adoption. We therefore opened our hearts to submit to His will! We agreed to meet up with the birth mom in St. Augustine.

It was crazy, because from the time we met her, we felt like there was a special bond between us. We really felt like this was our situation. She chose us as the parents. We were so excited! We made a couple of visits to see her before the delivery, and on December 07, 2014, a baby girl was born.

She was so beautiful! She had a full head of hair. She was a doll baby. We weren't in the clear just yet, though. God still had to work out some kinks. My wife, myself, and the birth parents were all at the hospital. The baby was born and everyone involved was in agreement with our game plan.

And then there was a hiccup.

The father's family members started coming to the hospital to see the baby. That *wasn't* part of the game plan! Keep in mind, no one had been there for the birth mother when she found herself in some unfortunate circumstances before the delivery. None of those people even cared to check on her. Now all of a sudden everybody had something to say about the new baby girl.

We had to go into complete prayer mode, because the enemy was definitely trying to stop this process. We knew we couldn't give him any leverage to do so. We called up our prayer warriors and told them to get to praying.

The father's parents were trying to convince him not to sign the legal papers. The birth mother and father knew it was in the best interest of the baby for them to sign over their rights. It was funny, because God had already told us that we were going to have to trust Him to the very end. God is not a man that He should lie. He surely wasn't lying about this either. They wrestled with signing the papers all the way. Then they finally signed them. Praise God!

We still weren't in the clear, though; we still had to come up with the rest of the money to complete the adoption. God used people who we least expected to help us pay the rest of the money off. Won't He do it??

9 BEFORE THE STORM

We moved on with our lives. Things were going well until my wife started noticing some issues of concern regarding the new baby. She started doing some research and that's when she started making appointments for the baby to be seen by different professionals. They came up with a couple of diagnoses. While all that was going on, we felt a tugging on our hearts to adopt again. This time, I was the one who felt like God was calling us to do so. My wife and I discussed it, and neither of us wanted our first adopted daughter to feel bad about being the only adopted child in the family.

We decided to go with a different agency this time, so we hooked up with a new one. We knew what we needed to do this time, because we had gone through this twice already. Guess what? Yes, you guessed right! We got a call from the agency saying we got matched.

We arranged to take a trip to meet the mom. She was due to give birth in May 2016. We met her and she fell in love with us. She was struggling with some issues, so we were a little concerned for the baby. Still, we knew this situation was orchestrated by God, so everything would be all good. We just had to trust Him through the process.

We attended frequent doctor's appointments to see the birth mother before the delivery. In May of 2016, a baby girl was born – perfectly healthy with all ten fingers and all ten toes. We were assured by the birth mom that the last person she had been with was a black guy. We were expecting a mixed baby, but again, we were open to whatever God wanted for our family. We met the birth mom's father in the hospital the day of the delivery. He knew we were expecting the baby to be mixed, because that is what his daughter had told him.

Well, the baby was born and he was the only one in the delivery room with his daughter. We were in the waiting room, anxious and praying everything was okay. The dad walked out of the delivery room with this weird look on his face. Then he proceeded to say, "I don't know how to say this, but that is a white baby." I guess he thought we were going to pass out or something or start screaming "No!" My wife and I just looked at each other and smiled. Then we told him that we were open to whatever the baby was. It was a very funny moment at the time.

It was tough for the mother to sign over her beautiful baby girl, but she did it. We brought her home from the hospital the next day. Life was grand!

Again, things were going well until my wife started to notice our older girl, who was by this time around a year and a half, being aggressive with the new baby. She also noticed her being aggressive with our younger son. She started observing her behavior a little more and noticed that she wasn't getting along with any of the other kids.

By this time, the other kids weren't too happy with her. My wife started telling me about some of the things that she had observed the older girl doing. I believed her, but I just hadn't seen anything out of the ordinary with my own eyes. This led to a lot of arguments and fights between my wife and me. She started to feel like I was taking the two-year-old's side over hers and that I wasn't supporting her to help fix the problem. I didn't agree with that at all.

By this time, our first adoptive child's behavior had gotten even worse, and we were worried for the other children's safety. We came to the conclusion that she just wasn't a good fit for our family. We believed she needed to be in a family with no siblings, where she was the only child. As hard as it was for all of us, we had to make a change. We decided that if we wanted to knit our family back together, the best thing to do was to find someone who would want to adopt her.

You talk about a test of your faith. This was a child whom we'd raised from a newborn baby. And now we had to give her up. It was a tough call for all of us. I was talking to a colleague at work about our circumstance, and she mentioned that one of our other co-workers might be interested in helping out with our toddler on the weekends. I talked to the other person, and she was delighted to assist. She owned a dance studio, so she was happy to have the child come on the weekends and offered to give her dance lessons for free. We started taking her to the dance studio, which Baby Girl liked. She then started staying the night with my co-worker on occasion.

My co-worker fell head-over-heels in love with her. My wife and I met with her to see if maybe she would be interested in adopting her. A little while later, my wife, who was understandably very conflicted, was a little hesitant about letting her go and started looking into other options for her. My wife felt like she still wanted to have contact with her. The coworker didn't want to keep having her go back and forth because it wasn't healthy for the two-year-old. So she said either she is going to stay or she has to go. I was in agreement with that idea, because I knew we could not have her in our house any longer. My wife was indecisive about it, but she knew we could no longer keep her in our home. Without sharing too many details, let me just say that her behavior was toxic to our marriage and to our other kids.

I know it sounds like my wife and I were just cruel human beings who took this child into our home and then gave up on her when things got rough, and I can understand you feeling that way. There are a lot of things I could say to justify our decision, but I just don't think it would be fair to a child to share details about her life in such a public way. Suffice it to say, this was a tough decision my wife and I felt like we had to make in the best interest of everyone involved. We grieved the loss of this child, but we believe she is in a great environment for which she is better suited today.

To be fair, my wife didn't feel like I supported her in that whole situation. I didn't agree with her then, but later I was able to admit that I wasn't as supportive as I could've been. It was just a lot to process in such a short period of time. I later apologized to my wife. She did such an amazing job caring for and loving her where she was. To me I felt like I was between a rock and a hard place, but we had to make the best decision for our family and for this little girl.

My wife and I both were in agreement with the baby leaving our home to live with my co-worker, who eventually adopted her. My wife never really had peace with the idea, because — as I mentioned earlier — she wanted to be able to see her every now and then. I didn't think that would be healthy for our other kids or the toddler. I felt like it was a God move that saved our marriage and family at that time. My family went to counseling after that whole situation, because it was not something you would ever have expected to happen and we needed help dealing with our feelings. My wife and I did both marriage counseling and individual counseling.

Figure 1-1 Me (front right) at three years old with my mother Bobbie Jean Terry; brother Jermaine & sister Shamika

Figure 1-2 Me (right) with Paul (center) and Jason (left) at a New Orleans Saints practice.

Figure 1-3 Me (left) with Mr. Harry and Jason.

I AM A KING

Figure 1-4 Me at a football game at Bay High School

Figure 1-5 Me (3rd from left) with my boys on my wedding day.

Figure 1-6 Me (2nd from left) with a few of my Navy friends in Spain.

Figure 1-7 Pee Wee football!

Figure 1-8 My student ID from St. Stanislaus Prep.

Figure 1-9 Me (left) with my cousin Xavier Lewis, who inspired me on the football field.

Figure 1-10 Me as a Navy Signalman on deployment to Europe.

10 MY ROAD TO DAMASCUS EXPERIENCE

About a month later, my wife and I were having a conversation and at one point, I mentioned how I had tried to toughen her up in the beginning of our marriage. She got really upset about it, because she felt like I had tried to change the individual she was. I felt like at that time I didn't understand the emotional support she was expecting from me. I felt like I didn't know how to connect with her emotionally. Yes, I had made progress over the years, but I guess it wasn't enough.

Then I said something along the lines of "It might take sixty years for me to get where you want me to be." I think for her, hearing that was the breaking point. With all that she had previously gone through, she felt like I had never valued who she was. Looking back, I think it was a combination of knowing I had tried to change her; her feeling like I had no ambition; the failed adoptions; her believing I didn't value who she was, and the lack of emotional connection. All of that was compounded by her having a sense that she had done everything right in her life as a believer and she still ended up in unfortunate circumstances.

Looking back now, I believe all those things combined to put her mind in a compromised place. Things and events happened so fast that she never had a chance to process it all. She came to me later and told me she needed a break from our marriage; that she needed to rethink our marriage.

I was caught off-guard with this one. I asked, "Are you saying to separate?"

I was shocked. I thought things had been good over our 11-year span of being together. I surely would never agree to a separation. I always preached that you can work anything out in marriage. She kept pushing for separation, so I finally gave in to it. I felt like I had no choice in the matter.

I can admit to saying some hurtful things to her as I was going through this situation. Those words came from a place of hurt, panic, and a lot of confusion. I felt like they were true, but I probably should not have said them. The power of the tongue is real. I had never been in a situation like this before in my life and I never could've imagined being in that place.

Looking back, I take full responsibility for not playing a more supportive role at times in the marriage, but I honestly never saw this coming. I believed the enemy found a crease and wiggled his way into my relationship with my wife.

From that day on, I was in the fight of my life. I'm not at liberty to talk about all that happened, but it was nothing I ever could have imagined us facing. My wife and I were divorced five months later.

I would never question my wife's love for me over that 11-year span; those were the most amazing years of my life. I can honestly say that I gave all my love, my heart, my sweat, and my soul for my family. Only my ex-wife can agree or disagree with that. This is my truth and my story. Even so, you should already know that there are always two sides to a story. I thank God, because He showed me things about me that I had no idea I had inside me. One of the things He showed me was that I had a lot of pride – pride that had been building up since I was a young boy. It was a sense of pride that made me feel like I was so special that God would not allow anything bad to happen to me. God had always showed me favor in everything I did.

I knew from the time I was little that there was something special about me. As I grew up, it was obvious. I'm not saying that in an arrogant way; I'm saying people's desire to connect with me was always evident. That was something I couldn't control, but it did build a sense of over-confidence within me. The Bible talks about pride coming before destruction in Proverbs 16:18. I can remember hearing about other people's marriage situations and how the husband did this or the wife did that. I could remember my thoughts on it like it was yesterday. They were similar to this, "That couldn't happen to me." "I'm glad I'm not like him." "I can't believe she or he did that to their spouse." Those were all prideful and judgmental responses to other people's situations. If you don't learn anything from this book learn this: don't ever put your mouth on another person's situation. When you do that, you sow a bad seed in your own life. No one is exempt from bad things happening to them. No one is exempt from going through challenges. Don't get it twisted and think it can't happen to you.

> If you don't learn anything from this book learn this: don't ever put your mouth on another person's situation.

You also have to understand that the tough or bad things that God allows you to go through are not meant to kill you. They are meant to make you stronger; build character; see what's in your heart, and help you grow in your relationship with Jesus. Don't ever look for God to pull you out of a situation; "… he has said, 'I will never leave you nor forsake you.'" (Heb. 13:5, ESV). God is always with us, but that doesn't exempt us from going through the process. He will not pull you out, but He will walk with you and pull you *through*. Sometimes God has to break you down to your knees to get your attention.

God is always talking; we're just not always listening. That's when He has to turn up the fire on us to get us to wake up.

11 MY EYES ARE OPENED

These statements I know to be true:

- Life is tough!
- Marriage is challenging!
- Love can be complicated.
- The devil is deceiving.
- God is real.

I speak this from experience! God had to allow me to hit rock-bottom to get His message across to me. I lost my marriage; I went to jail (bet you didn't see *that* coming!); I lost my job, and I'm pretty sure everything else would have followed that same trend if my eyes hadn't been opened.

I'd never been to jail before in my life. In the previous chapter, I mentioned that I was finally beginning to understand that I had way too much pride in myself. Going to jail was an experience I believe God used to teach me humility. It is my firm belief that spending a night in jail is a perfect way to teach a person humility. In jail, society views you as a criminal. You could be the president of the United States, but if you're in jail, you are looked at as a criminal just like everyone else in there. You are a nothing more than a number and regardless of what the law of the land officially says, once you land in jail, you are (for all intents and purposes) guilty until proven innocent.

Even in that situation, God was showing me favor. There can be no doubt that this was a circumstance where I definitely I wanted *out*, but as I mentioned in the previous chapter, God's presence was with me, pulling me *through*. It just wasn't time for me to come out of the fire just yet.

I know I made a big leap from the previous chapter, and you're probably wondering what you missed. Let me fill you in.

What landed me in jail was a bad decision.

I left my job at the spine center to pursue a job at a brewery. I had been gone from my previous job for about a month when everything happened. The doctor I worked for just before leaving was writing a common prescription for my ex-wife. That morning she noticed that she had run out of the medication, so she asked me if I could get someone to call it in for her.

I said, "I can't get anyone to do that." Then I said, "I can just call it in; it shouldn't be a problem." I was also thinking I could get some brownie points with her if I called it in.

To be honest with you, I felt the Holy Spirit telling me not to make that call, but I ended up calling the prescription in. As soon as I hung up the phone, I knew I had just made a big mistake.

We have to understand that God has given us the Holy Spirit as our helper. When you ignore God and do what you want to do, it will always put you in comprising situations. I knew I had messed up once I hung up the phone, so I called the pharmacy to see if they had the prescription ready. The pharmacist who answered the phone asked me if I was the one who called the prescription in. I said yes then he said that he called the spine center and they told him that I no longer worked there. He then said that he was going to call the police and that I could get jail time for fraudulently calling in a prescription. At that time, I was scared and paranoid. I couldn't think or focus. All I could think about was that I was about to go to jail and how bad this was going to look on me, my family, and the doctor.

The whole time I was dealing with these feelings, the devil was trying to convince me to kill myself. But I knew that wasn't even an option. I had to remind myself that God is a forgiving God and that He loves me. I reminded the devil that he was a liar. I decided that I needed to stand up and be a man and take responsibility for my actions.

One hour later, I got a knock on the door and it was the police. They escorted me right to jail. I believe God orchestrated that situation to happen because He really needed to talk to me without any distractions. When you are locked up like that, there are absolutely no distractions around you.

When you're locked up in jail, the devil wants to mess with you. He knows he has you exactly where he wants you – locked up so you can't be effective to the outside world. I can't speak for anyone else, but he was wrong about *me* on that one. I ministered Jesus, hope, and purpose to everyone God put on my heart to talk to in there. They let me out the next day and dropped the charges. Praise God! When I was walking out to be released, I literally received a standing ovation.

Any time God sits you down in isolation, you better believe He wants to talk. He has been trying to talk to you for a while, but you were too busy to listen. That experience was ordained by God. Obviously, He didn't want me to call in a prescription I didn't have the right to call in, but I believe He orchestrated what happened afterwards so I could be in that place alone with Him. God clearly told me that I put something very dear to my heart before Him one too many times. I felt like God was saying that I had put my ex-wife ahead of Him far too often. I knew I had done this, so I repented on the spot. I promised God I would never compromise my relationship with Him ever again.

I wouldn't wish jail on any man. That place is not for anyone! I cannot understand why people keep going back! I'm sorry, but that one time woke me *all the way up*! That was a life-changing experience for me.

As if being in lock-up wasn't bad enough, about a month later, I lost my new job.

I feel like God used that job to teach me humility, too.

The first way it accomplished that was that I had to take a pay cut to work a three-month seasonal position for only $15 per hour, in the hope of getting hired on full-time for $32 per hour. I really hated the job, but it was what God blessed me with for that time and it was paying the bills. That job was nothing like I expected it to be. The work environment was hot; they treated us like worker bees, and the internal politics there were terrible. It was a very humbling experience for me; I had never ever imagined myself working a blue-collar labor job.

Another way I learned humility while I was there was through another seasonal worker like myself, who was trying to get a full-time position. He lied on me to a supervisor. The supervisor gave me a bad evaluation for that week. I didn't even fight it, because the supervisor was already convinced that I was wrong and they had already collaborated to come up with a story to justify it. I took that hit, prayed for both of them, and kept it moving. I was already convinced that being at the company was not the will of God for my life and I did not want to be there anyways.

I knew God had me in the fire for a reason. When you're in the fire, know that God is in control of the thermostat. The fire was burning my impurities off so when God was done with me I would shine brighter than ever before. When my ex-wife and I went after that job, we were stuck on how much money I could make for the family. We'd never ever chased after money before and God has always provided our needs.

My ex-wife made a good point regarding why the job could've been great for our family, but I wasn't really feeling the sacrifice it was going to take to get the money.

When you're in the fire, know that God is in control of the thermostat.

The door opened for the job after two years of waiting and I knew it was God who opened it. Once I was in and observed how things were done there, I knew it wasn't for me long term. I believe the purpose of that position was to allow all the unfortunate events that happened to happen. Because of what I was going through in my marriage, I was never in a good place mentally to give the job my best efforts. It was the perfect job for me to have at that moment in my life. I felt that way because with all that I went through while working there, I really should've been fired early in my stint. But God kept me there for His purpose.

There wasn't a day that went by that I didn't feel God's presence with me. God would send random people to me with a Word from God. It was crazy!!! That's why I have to trust God's plan for my life and not my own. That situation could not have been planned out any more perfectly than it was. Trust me when I say that.

More than anything, I hate that my marriage ended the way it did, but I felt like my hands were tied on that. I believe God can and will restore and heal my ex-wife and myself if we have faith that He will. We have to go through the healing process though – "And without faith it is impossible to please him, for whoever would draw near to God must believe that he exists and that he rewards those who seek him." (Heb. 11:6, ESV)

This is my journey and my story! Jesus said that it is finished! Our story was finished when He died on the cross for our sins. I just have to follow the blueprint that He has provided for my life. His will is the perfect will for our lives.

12 COMING OUT OF THE WILDERNESS

Listen to me when I tell you this: I would not wish divorce on any man. It's literally like experiencing the death of a loved one. If you don't go through all the right steps, you will never heal completely from it. I thank God that He placed brothers in my life to help walk me through it – brothers who went through it themselves and knew all the emotions, thoughts, and trauma of going through a divorce. Those brothers really helped me. If you are one of them and you're reading this book, you know who you are. I thank you from the bottom of my heart for all your love, support, and prayers.

Though this was a big one, I thank God for it. I learned how to love without strings attached. I learned how not to judge other people's situations. I learned how powerful the tongue is (the power of words – see Proverbs 18:21). I learned that pride comes before the fall (see Proverbs 16:18). I learned not to ever take the people you love for granted – don't ever take a break from telling and showing them that you love them. I was reminded that the devil hates marriages and believers of Christ. The thief (devil) comes to kill, steal and destroy, but Jesus came that they may have life and may have it abundantly. (John 10:10)

This has been a bittersweet season in my life. I lost the most amazing person that has ever been in my life, but I found my first love – Christ. Not that I ever lost Him. I just lost my main focus on Him in the grand scheme of life, marriage, and raising kids. I sit back and I think how easy that is to do. I clearly understand what the apostle Paul meant when he said he would rather you stay unmarried like him because you can focus everything on God. Then he came back and said, "but if you can't control yourself, then marry." (1 Cor. 7:8-9, paraphrased)

It's easy for a husband to lose his focus on God while raising a family, because he wants to give his wife everything she needs and wants. As a husband, you want to listen and take all her advice in any situation, but you have to have balance even in that. What also makes it hard is that you can see your wife, but you can't actually *see* God. I felt like for a lot of the moves we made, we both heard from God on them. I feel like there were a lot of little decisions where I allowed her to have what she wanted. I never wanted to seem like I controlled her, but the enemy can deceive a person into believing that.

It's funny how the devil uses people to plant seeds in other people's minds. It's an old trick that was used even in the beginning — in the book of Genesis — that still works amazingly in this world today.

I read a book by John Bevere called *Victory in the Wilderness: Growing Strong in Dry Times*. I believe that book was God-sent just for me in that season of my life. God knows what we needs and when we need it. This book blessed me so much. It seemed like every time I opened it up, there was a fresh Word straight from God's mouth just for me.

I decided to start praying, fasting, and reading the Word every day. I knew that was the only way I was going to make it through that storm alive. I contacted all the men of God in my circle who I knew would ride with me through anything, and asked them to be praying and fasting with me. Not one of them hesitated to stand in prayer with me. I truly believe God hears prayers. As hard as things were for me, God always found a way to remind me of His love for me. Sometimes it would be through a song. Like I said earlier, even at work He would send people that would have a Word from Him for me. He also used my brothers (through text or phone calls, etc.) to encourage me.

My goal was not to let bitterness get in my spirit towards the person I had once loved with all my heart. It took her rejecting me time after time for me to realize that this lady didn't love me the same way anymore. I realized that she was rejecting me to protect herself. Sometimes we hurt people unintentionally so we won't get hurt ourselves. I get it now! God started slowly healing me one day at a time. I would have my good days and some bad ones, too. As a result of that season and that circumstance, I really can say that I know what the Peace of God feels like.

13 GOD'S LOVE

My next steps in life can only be led by God. I trust Him 100% to direct me in His will for my life. I heard a saying that goes, "Anything you put before God, you better be willing to lose." Well, now I know that it is true. Think about this: the highest level of love Jesus expressed was dying on the cross for us. God often references His relationship to the church (us) as that of a groom towards His bride. Jesus laid His life on the line for us (the church). Men and women of God, our calling as a spouse is to lay it all on the line for our spouse. I'm so hard on myself when I consider that I did that, but I didn't have balance in it. Do you see how hard that can be when God has called us to love them in that way?

I am a person who learns from my mistakes because I never want to have to retake the same test in life again. This was the big one for me! It almost took me under, but God believed in me. If it wasn't for His grace and mercy, I probably would've done something I would've regretted for the rest of my life. Jesus just kept reminding me of His love. That is one thing I cannot deny – that Jesus loves me.

One lesson about the wilderness is this: you are either going to die in the wilderness or you will make it to the Promised Land. I don't know about you, but I'm determined to make it to the Promised Land. I have a new perspective on life now. Life is about making choices and decisions, and once they're made you have to deal with the consequences. You noticed I didn't say *live with them*, because you don't have to live with a bad decision for the rest of your life. That defeats the purpose of

Life is about making choices and decisions, and once they're made you have to deal with the consequences….
Everyone is just one stupid decision away from losing it all.

what Jesus did on the cross for us. He died to save us and once we accept Him into our hearts, we can live the abundant life He promises us. Don't ever look at yourself as more than what you are. Everyone is just one stupid decision away from losing it all.

14 THE DEVIL IS AFTER YOUR MIND

The battlefield is in the mind. I know we all have heard that saying once or twice in our lives. I'm here to tell you that the battle is real. The enemy will sow a seed in your mind, and once that seed gets water, here comes the harvest! Regarding the end of my marriage, I was caught off-guard because I had never been in a similar situation before. My mind had no idea what was on the horizon, but I was in for the ride of my life.

The seed had been planted in my marriage. Never in a million years could I have ever seen this one coming. That's when the roller coaster started spinning. Things started happening so quickly, I didn't even have time to ask myself, "Did that just happen?"

After several unexpected situations occurred, my mind was in overdrive. I didn't know what to say or think, or who to ask. By this time, the devil had set up camp in my mind. The situations had caused my mind to go to places it had never visited before. That is when I had no choice but to turn to God through His Word, prayer, and music.

The struggle was real. The enemy started building up scenarios and situations that really had me ready to lose my mind. I was trying to fight with the Word of God, but because I had allowed the enemy to set up camp in my mind, I was losing the battle. The Word was doing its job, but I kept allowing the enemy to play devil's advocate with me. At this point, I started having trouble distinguishing between the Holy Spirit and the devil. I was struggling! The enemy tormented me for six months with thoughts, pictures, and words… until I totally surrendered my mind, body, and soul to God. Meaning, I decided to go *all in* with Jesus – withholding nothing!

Don't get me wrong; I will slip up at times and struggle. I will miss the mark now and then. Even so, I have a better understanding of who Jesus is and what

He came to earth to bring. He came to bring grace and truth. I started learning more about our adversary the devil and that he is the accuser of the brethren. By putting more of God's Word in my mind, it washed the enemy and his home straight out. Yes, I still struggle at times with certain unwelcome thoughts, but I know how to fight. Greater is He who is in me than He who is in the world. (1 John 4:4)

You can't stop a thought from popping into your head, but you can either accept it or rebuke it. We have to understand that when we gave our lives to Jesus, nothing changed in our mind. We have to allow the Word of God to change our mindset and our thinking. If you don't, your walk with Jesus will be very challenging. The battle starts in the mind and ends there, too.

15 THE DEVIL – THE ACCUSER OF THE BRETHREN (TIM. 4:13)

The devil comes to kill, steal, and destroy. (John 10:10) He doesn't come for any other reason. He uses many different tactics in this arena and all are very effective. The devil continually tries to plant bad seeds in your mind using your feelings. He uses the feelings of shame, guilt, embarrassment, and worthlessness as tools to distract you from what God's Word says you are. He knows that if he can get water on those seeds, the harvest will bring forth destruction in your life. Then he knows that he can easily get you out of the will of God.

When you have those feelings, you literally feel like you are no good to anyone. Let's take Judas, for example: Judas betrayed Jesus! Immediately after he betrayed Jesus he felt shame, guilt, and embarrassment. Judas allowed those feeling to overtake his body, his mind, and his soul. At that point, he felt useless to everyone, so he killed himself. We know that Jesus would've forgiven Judas, but for Judas himself, the pain was too overwhelming.

The devil uses those same tricks today, but if you really have a relationship with Jesus you should know that Jesus came to bring grace and truth, not to condemn. (John 1:17) God's grace is something that we don't deserve. You have to believe that you can be restored from any mistake you've made or will make in your life. His grace is sufficient for you; His strength is made perfect in our weakness. (2 Cor. 12:9)

The best example of God's restoration power is Peter. Because of fear, Peter denied God not once but *three* times in front of many. I'm sure afterwards Peter felt shame, guilt, and embarrassment. Peter had a true revelation of who Jesus was and he knew who he was in Christ. He wasn't going to let his mistake stop him from doing what God had called him to do. We have to understand that feelings come and they go; you can't trust them. Peter didn't, and God restored him. After that, Peter went harder after God than ever before. God's love and grace have the power to heal and restore.

You have to believe that God will restore you if you trust Him. Let's look at Job. He lost it all and never cursed God. He had people in his ear saying so much negative stuff, but Job stood firm in what he believed about his God. Job was not perfect; he was just like you and me, yet God called him blameless and upright. (Job 1:8) Job did sin, but he acknowledged his sin and repented to God for it.

We have to know that we can repent from sin and move on. Repentance has to be from the heart. King David was considered a man after God's own heart, but to be honest, he did some really bad things in his life. One thing about King David was that we never see him committing the same sin twice. That tells you that David's heart for God was so strong that he wanted only what God wanted for his life. King David knew how to repent first, then he evaluated his experience and learned not to make the same mistake again. "You will seek me and find me when you seek me with all your heart." (Jer. 29:13, NIV)

16 THE HEALING PROCESS

Anytime you go through a traumatic event in your life, such as divorce or the loss of a loved one, there is an important healing process you must go through in order to move on and live a healthy life.

Like I said before, when you go through a divorce, it's just like experiencing the death of a loved one. You go through the same grieving process. You have to remember that when you marry, you come into a spiritual covenant with your spouse. "For this reason a man will leave his father and mother and be united to his wife, and the two will become one flesh." (Matt. 19:5, NIV) In marriage, you become one with your spouse.

The Bible teaches that woman came from the rib of a man. When a man and woman marry in holy matrimony, spiritually the man is complete because he has found his missing rib. They then become one and a holy covenant is made between the two. When a divorce takes place, there is a breaking that takes place in the soul of each person.

These people have promised to give their body, heart, and soul to one another. Losing that other person is therefore no different from losing a loved one to death. That loved one has made a special mark on your soul that can't be erased. They have invested their life into loving you and making you a better person. Then, for whatever reason, they are no longer a part of your life. At that moment, you might experience feelings of hurt, pain, confusion, loss, or even abandonment because that partner is no longer in your life.

There is a grieving process that many people go through before finding their healing (denial, anger, bargaining, depression, and acceptance). It's okay to go through that process, but you can't allow yourself to get stuck in any of those stages. It's very important to heal properly after going through a divorce. If you don't heal properly, you will set yourself up for failure in your next relationships.

I've talked to many people who have gone through divorce and I've noticed a pattern with each situation. Let me say this and make it clear about divorce: everyone is a victim and a perpetrator. Each person played a role and part in the situation. In saying that, each person has to go through their own healing process. The only way to get proper healing is to go through Jesus who is a healer. Please understand that if you run to anything other than your source (Jesus), you will not heal properly and you will suffer for the rest of your life from that hurt you've experienced. The hurt and pain that have been inflicted on you by people will and can control you for the rest of your life if you don't heal properly.

It's natural for us as humans to search for coping mechanisms when faced with a traumatic situation. Based on my research, the three main things people typically turn to after facing a traumatic situation are drugs, sex, and alcohol. Those are three things that can take away the pain and hurt, but they are only going to give you temporary relief. If you continue down that road, it only leads to destruction.

The best option you can choose is turning to Jesus. Just like a fish needs water and a plant needs soil, we need God. Jesus is our source and our means of access to the abundant life here on earth. There is no other way to live a great life here on earth without Him. In my situation, I had no other choice but to turn to Jesus. I had tried all the other options before in my life and they had only led to destruction, an unfulfilled void, and more hurt and pain. When I finally decided to fully give it to Jesus, He was there with open arms, ready to take my burdens. That's when my healing process started. He began healing me from the inside out.

It's always a tough journey when walking with Jesus, because we live in this flesh. There is a battle going on between our flesh and our spirit. Because we live in this world, we have the temptations of the world right at our finger tips.

When you decide to walk solely with Jesus for anything, you better get ready to battle. You are not battling for victory, because we have already won the battle against the devil. Jesus defeated the enemy when

He died on the cross for our sins. If you don't turn to Jesus for your healing and instead try to heal with temporary fixes such as sex, drugs, and alcohol, that's like trying to put a Band-Aid on a shotgun wound: it's not going to work!! What happens is that eventually the wound gets infected and gangrene tries to set in. Once gangrene sets in, the wound's body tissue starts to die; then you have no choice but to have it cut off. It's vital that you take proper care of that wound so that it can heal correctly. If not treated properly, that injury has the potential to kill you because it spreads to other areas of your body. Then it eventually affects your heart.

The healing process is not a one-step process. You have to take it one day at a time. I say that because you will have setbacks, but you have to continue in the Word of God to make it to the end. You will have times where you will feel like God is taking a nap on you and there will be times where you have to encourage yourself in the Lord. Even when we don't feel His presence, we have to remember that He said He will never leave us nor forsake us. (Heb. 13:5) In your healing process, the devil your adversary will be extremely busy playing mind games with you. Like I said in chapter 14, the battlefield is in the mind. You will have to continue to remind yourself of who God says you are and not the lies of what the enemy will try and plant in your head.

My pastor Russ Austin said this, "You are what you love, not what you think." That's such a true statement, because the devil will try and plant all kinds of false and negative thoughts about you in your head. This is very important to know as you go through your healing process. Make sure you are surrounded by like-minded people – sound, spiritual people who have gone through what you are experiencing. Those are the only people who will fully understand the emotions you are feeling and the thoughts you are having, and they will also know all the tricks the enemy will try and play on your mind. I live by this saying, "What we go through is not for us, but it's to help the people God places in our lives that are going through the same things we went through." In the end, God gets the glory for bringing us out, but in His timing.

Our testimony should be a witness of what Jesus has done in our lives. I tell people we shouldn't have to hit people across the head with the Bible to get them to believe. I know Jesus is real by what He has brought me out of. I feel like if more of us shared our testimony with others, then they would see that there was nothing we did to be where we are – it was all God. Then God would get all the glory!

We are saved by His grace for His purpose. "They overcame him [satan] by the blood of the Lamb and by the word of their testimony…" (Rev. 12:11a, NIV) Satan is defeated every time a believer tells his or story of redemption.

Satan is defeated every time a believer tells his or story of redemption.

17 MY NEXT CHAPTER

As I turn the page to the next chapter of my life, I can't help but reflect. I tell people that we have to evaluate our experiences. I've heard people say that experience is the best teacher, but if you don't evaluate your experience, you will continue to make the same mistakes over and over again. I therefore say life is the best teacher.

Life has the ability to make you or break you. Life tests you whether you want the test or not. When that test comes, you can: (1) ignore the test, (2) take the test and pass it, or (3) take the test and fail it. Regardless of which choice you make, the test is going to affect your life in some way or fashion. My prayer is that every test you take in life helps to mature you in a way that you learn from it. Then you will be able to be a blessing to those God places in your life for you to be a blessing to.

I will reiterate this, "What you go through in life is not for you, but it's for you to be able to help the hundreds of people who will go through the same thing you went through." God strategically placed the right people in my life who helped me get through my storm (divorce). They were men who had gone through the same things I was going through; men led by God with the Word of God in their mouth sitting on their tongues. My storm didn't catch God by surprise. He could've changed the narrative of my story, but He allowed me to go through it. God will never make us do anything against our own will. Would God be a loving God if He made us do things we didn't want to do? If He made us do only what He wanted us to do? When things get messed up, we would try and blame Him, just like Adam tried to do when Eve ate from the tree then gave him a piece of the apple:

> And they heard the sound of the Lord God walking in the garden in the cool of the day, and Adam and his wife hid themselves from

the presence of the Lord God among the trees of the garden.

Then the Lord God called to Adam and said to him, "Where *are* you?"

So he said, "I heard Your voice in the garden, and I was afraid because I was naked; and I hid myself."

And He said, "Who told you that you *were* naked? Have you eaten from the tree of which I commanded you that you should not eat?"

Then the man said, "The woman whom You gave *to be* with me, she gave me of the tree, and I ate."

(Gen. 3:8-12, NKJV)

God knows how we are and how we like to shift the blame from ourselves to others. I want to encourage you to be a man or woman and take responsibility for your actions! We can fool the people around us, but we can't fool God.

Do you think when God asked Adam and Eve, "Where are you?" that He didn't know where they were? Of course He knew where they were! He just wanted them to acknowledge what they did and take responsibility for their actions.

Out of fear, we lie and don't tell the truth because we're afraid of the consequences that come afterwards. And sometimes we lie so we won't hurt the people we love the most. We're all guilty of it at one point or another in our lives. Again, we can fool everybody around us, but we can't fool God. God is omnipotent (all powerful); omniscient (knowing everything), and omnipresent (He is everywhere at once). God is love! It's impossible to love another person if you don't know the love of God. His love is unconditional, meaning that it doesn't matter what we do against Him; what we say about Him, or how we treat Him, He loves us no matter what!

When you love someone, you are in constant pursuit of them. Jesus is always pursuing us and He will continue to pursue you every day until you surrender your life to Him. He loves you that much!

Jesus is always pursuing us and He will continue to pursue you every day until you surrender your life to Him. He loves you that much!

18 PURPOSE

1. We all have a purpose for being on this earth.

God created us all for a purpose. When God created you, He had a specific task in mind that He wanted to use you for. What happens a lot of times is people walk through life not knowing what their purpose is. When you don't know the purpose of something, you tend to misuse it. Example: I buy a box of sharpened pencils. If I didn't know the purpose of a pencil, I might just start breaking them in half. I might go through a whole box of pencils, just breaking them one by one. Then someone just so happens to see me and comes and tells me, "Pencils are made to write with." I would then stop breaking the pencils and start writing with them. After learning the use of the pencils, I would start using them for their purpose. It would take someone who knows the function of the pencils to tell me that they had a purpose. Jesus has the blueprint to your life. He holds the key to your purpose. As you pursue Him in your faith walk, He will reveal your purpose to you. God puts desires in your heart. God can and will give you the desires of your heart if you seek after Him. "Delight thyself also in the Lord and he shall give thee the desires of thine heart." (Psalm 37:4, KJV)

Think about something in your life you said and believed you would never do, for example: getting married. I know men who have said, "I will never get married." Then one day that same person meets an amazing woman. That woman is everything he needs in a partner. Next thing you know, he's ready to take her to the altar. I believe God put the desire in his heart to want to marry that woman.

2. Our purpose is also connected to people.

Not only is your purpose linked to the people in your life today, but to those who have left your life, as well.

Everyone in your life has a role to play. That role could be good or bad! The people who aren't still in your life today have played their role and moved on. This scripture is for anyone who is not still in your life. "They went out from us, but they did not really belong to us. For if they had belonged to us, they would have remained with us; but their going showed that none of them belonged to us." (1 John 2:19, NIV) Now, you can take that and apply it to any situation you like.

It's so important to stay connected to like-minded people. You are the company you hang with. That's not being judgmental! It's a true statement! I have great friends I talk to who aren't believers, but our conversations are superficial. I love them like brothers. We don't share the same beliefs, but we can still learn from one another. I don't push what I believe on them and they definitely don't try and convince me that what I believe is wrong. God can use anything, any person, or any voice to speak to us. If God can use a donkey to speak to Balaam in Numbers 22:28, He can use anything He well pleases to speak to us.

I encourage you to stay connected to positive people in your life. Don't just let *anyone* speak into your life. Just because someone talks to you every day, smiles in your face, and hangs out with you doesn't mean they have your best interest in mind. You could find out that they were jealous of you the whole time and wanted something you had.

It's important that we find our purpose in life. It's not an easy thing to do, but if you start early, I believe God will reveal it to you early in your life. Let me make this statement: you will not find your purpose outside of knowing Christ. I'm going to say this because I believe it – it's literally *impossible* to do so. You have to remember that God has the blueprint to your life. He created you! He knew you before you were in your mother's womb (Jer. 1:5). The sooner we know our purpose, the more likely it is that we will avoid unnecessary heartache and pain.

One of those things could be finding the right job for yourself. If we knew our purpose, we wouldn't just be working jobs just to work them! We would want to work jobs that

You will not find your purpose outside of knowing Christ.

are connected to our purpose. Don't get me wrong; sometimes you just have to get a job because you have responsibilities. Even in that, if you know your purpose you can use that job to help fulfill it. You will not always love your purpose or whatever you are doing that's connected to it. You have to understand that when you accepted Christ into your life, you gave your life to Him. Your purpose is inextricably linked to what He has called you to do for the Kingdom. In the end, He gets the glory and your biggest payout is in heaven. "Behold, I am coming quickly, and My reward is with Me, to give to each one as is his work." (Rev. 22:12, BSB)

Sometimes we find our purpose through trial and error. I told you: finding your purpose isn't easy or fun, but it's worth it. I feel like I've found what God has called me to do. I am here to share God's Word with young people. What better way to practice than with my own sons and daughter? Your kids should be your first responsibility to lead in the right direction. Sometimes leading your own kids can be more challenging than leading other people. It's probably not until your kids are adults that they will see you as something other than their parents.

The best advice I can give to anyone struggling leading their own kids is to just walk out the life you want them to follow in front of them. They're not going to follow what you say; they're watching what you *do*. They're like little sponges! They soak up whatever they see in front of them: the music you listen to; the words that come out of your mouth; how you dress; how you treat others, and what you watch on TV. It's not always an easy task to do. Don't ever forget that YOU ARE HUMAN. Don't beat yourself up because your children aren't where you would want them to be right now. And definitely don't let that stop you from doing what you know God has called you to do outside of your kids.

I learned that we have to trust God with everything we have, and that includes our kids. He is the one who gave us the little angels!! "Jesus said, 'Let the little children come to me, and do not hinder them, for the kingdom of heaven belongs to such as these.'" (Matt. 19:14, NIV) Jesus is telling us that He loves and cares about your children too. He is interested and invested in every area of your life, and He understands your needs, wants, feelings, emotions, and pains. God came to the earth as man in the flesh, and He experienced everything we will experience or have experienced, so whatever you are going through, Jesus understands and He has compassion for you. He's your heavenly father and He loves you! In the end, love wins!!!

Revelation 1:5 assures us that Jesus Christ "… is the faithful witness, the firstborn from the dead, and the ruler of the kings of the earth." (NIV) We are the kings of the earth. Jesus is the king of kings. Let's walk in the authority He has given us.

"I AM A KING!"

19 THE ONLY WAY WE ARE GOING TO MAKE IT TO THE PROMISED LAND IS TOGETHER

> "Surely none of the men who came up out of Egypt, from twenty years old and upward, shall see the land that I swore to give to Abraham, to Isaac, and to Jacob, because they have not wholly followed me, none except Caleb… and Joshua…, for they have wholly followed the LORD."
>
> (Num 32:11-12, ESV)

Our lives are governed by seasons. The great thing about seasons is that they change. For example, we have four seasons: winter, summer, fall, and spring. In the states like New York, they sometimes have brutal winters and we know that after winter comes spring.

You can't fully prepare for winter, because you don't know how bad it's going to be. There's only so much you can do to prepare for it, so you have to wait until winter actually gets here to find out exactly how bad it will be. The only way to find that out is by reading the weather in the paper, and/or listening to the weatherman on the radio/news. Regardless of how bad winter is, what gives you hope is spring, because you know that the springtime is the best time of the year to explore New York. In your mind, you know if you survive winter, you will get to experience spring. That's very similar to what we go through when we come against a storm in our lives.

When you're in a storm and are going through something challenging, you have to allow Jesus to be your weatherman; your faith is your hope to make it out of the storm. If you don't have faith in Jesus that you will make it out, you will have no hope. Without hope, people die before their time! That's the reason people are dying so quickly in the world today. They don't have any hope or they do have hope, but it's in the wrong things.

If you put your hope in anything other than Jesus, the chances of you living a purposeful life are slim to none. You noticed I didn't say *happy life*? I said *purposeful*, because we were placed on this earth by God for His purpose. When you are living a purposeful life, happiness comes naturally. Just think: if everyone in this world lived their life to help others find their purpose, the world would definitely be a better place. Instead, we've become a world where most of us only care about what others can do for us.

Notice that Joshua and Caleb were the only two spies that brought back a good report and believed that God would help them succeed. Without a doubt, they believed and trusted God's Word that they could possess the land. The only problem was that they now had to convince the children of Israel that they could do it:

> If the LORD delights in us, he will bring us into this land and give it to us, a land that flows with milk and honey. Only do not rebel against the LORD. And do not fear the people of the land, for they are bread for us. Their protection is removed from them, and the LORD is with us; do not fear them.
>
> (Num. 14:8-9, ESV)

Joshua and Caleb had a different spirit than everyone else in the camp. Their attitude was that if God said it, then we can do it, and there is nothing that can stop us. The next goal was getting the people's faith in line with theirs. We know the Word of God says, "... faith comes from hearing, and hearing by the word of Christ." (Rom. 10:17, NASB). The only way to build someone's faith is through teaching them the Word of God.

I believe Joshua and Caleb just started preaching the Word of God to the people; built up their faith, and encouraged them in the Lord, and once everyone was on board, they went and took the land. You noticed they didn't try and do it alone; neither should we.

Through my wilderness experience, God dealt with me. The wilderness experience was not to kill me; it was to humble me; to test me to see what was in my heart, and to see if I would keep His commandments. Know that your wilderness experience is to prepare you for the Promised Land. You will need other believers to rally with you so you can get there together. That's the reason for this book. I'm here to encourage you in the Lord. Don't die in your wilderness! God told me to tell you that the Promised Land is yours to take. God didn't bring you out of Egypt for you to die in the wilderness. Jesus died so you could have life and life more abundantly. (John 10:10)

What has God called you to do? What is holding you back from doing it? God has given you gifts and talents for you to help build up His kingdom. What are you doing with those gifts and talents? There are people out in the world who are depending on you to walk in your purpose so you can help them find *their* purpose.

I was talking to a guy at the store and he asked me a question: "Where do you think the most money is in the world is?"

I responded, "Where?"

"In the cemetery," he said. He further explained, "because people have died with gifts, talents, and ideals that they didn't do anything with." I say that to say your gifts and talents were given to you by God for a reason. It costs money to build the kingdom of God. I truly believe if you take care of God's business, He will bless yours.

>
> **I truly believe if you take care of God's business, He will bless yours.**

I told myself I will not be on my deathbed with any regrets of what I could've or should've done with my gifts and talents. The worst that could happen is that I try something and it doesn't work, but at least I will know that I tried! Let the next year of your life be about you pursuing the things that God has placed on your heart for years. For those ideas and dreams that have died, bring them back to life with your faith in the next year of your existence. The faith of the people Joshua and Caleb led to the Promised Land was dead, but Joshua and Caleb's faith resurrected their faith and they took the land. I encourage you to find other believers and align your faith with their faith and come out of your wilderness.

If you don't do it now, the next year will be a continuation of the last. Now is the time!!

I take this opportunity to remind you again that Jesus Christ "… is the faithful witness, the firstborn from the dead, and the ruler of the kings of the earth." (NIV) *We* are the kings of the earth, and Jesus is the king of kings. You have authority in Him, and you should be walking in it. Why? For this reason:

"YOU ARE A KING!!"

About the Author

Antonio Maxwell Benton is currently a barber and works at a Jun's Barbershop in Jacksonville, Florida. A devoted father to his three beautiful children, he loves working with the youth, sharing his life experiences. He currently attends Southpoint Community Church and has a heart to see people grow in Christ and find their purpose.

Antonio strongly believes in people getting the correct counsel in whatever situation they're in. He encourages people to seek counseling from people in the faith; professionals, and those who have gone through the same thing you are going through.

Antonio's desire for helping people stems from all the many people who have helped him along his journey through life. He loves relating to people through conversation; imparting; receiving; learning, and growing in Christ.

One day, Antonio hopes to speak to many and share his life story to help others on their journey.

Though divorced, the author desires to someday be married again so he can apply all he has learned in life to his next marriage. He loves enjoying time with family and friends, but is quick to clarify that his definition of *family* is this reply that Jesus gave when told that his family was waiting outside to see Him – "He replied to him, 'Who is My mother and who are My brothers?' Pointing to His disciples He said, 'Here are My mother and My brothers. For whoever does the will of My Father in heaven is My brother and sister and mother.'" (Matt. 12:48-50, BSB)

For speaking engagements and book club discussions, Antonio can be reached at:

- Email: antoniobenton@aol.com
- Instagram: @Iamantoniomaxwell
- Facebook: Antonio Maxwell

www.ingramcontent.com/pod-product-compliance
Lightning Source LLC
Chambersburg PA
CBHW070502100426
42743CB00010B/1727